RYAN'S
ESSENTIAL OUTLINES
OF
THE FEDERAL RULES OF
EVIDENCE

RYAN'S
ESSENTIAL OUTLINES
OF
THE FEDERAL RULES OF
EVIDENCE

▼

2005–2006 Student Edition

Daniel P. Ryan

iUniverse, Inc.

New York Lincoln Shanghai

RYAN'S ESSENTIAL OUTLINES OF THE FEDERAL
RULES OF EVIDENCE
2005–2006 Student Edition

iUniverse books may be ordered through booksellers or by contacting:

iUniverse
2021 Pine Lake Road, Suite 100
Lincoln, NE 68512
www.iuniverse.com
1-800-Authors (1-800-288-4677)

ISBN-13: 978-0-595-36554-8 (pbk)
ISBN-13: 978-0-595-80985-1 (ebk)
ISBN-10: 0-595-36554-X (pbk)
ISBN-10: 0-595-80985-5 (ebk)

Printed in the United States of America

CONTENTS

PREFACE

This book provides numerous outlines which can be employed over an entire fifteen-week law school Evidence or Advanced Evidence course and is designed for use by members of the judiciary, practitioners, law professors and law students as a review of the essential elements of the Federal Rules of Evidence.

This text consists of outlines I have compiled over ten years of teaching Evidence for continuing judicial education programs for the National Judicial College, the Michigan Judicial Institute, South Dakota Judicial Conference, Kansas Municipal Judges Conference, the Nevada State Bar, Nevada District Judges Association, the Pacific Islands Legal Institute, and as an Adjunct Professor of Law at the University of Detroit-Mercy, Ave Maria Law School, and for Evidence and Advanced Evidence courses I've taught at Cooley Law School. I would like to thank my former students over the years that have made it a wonderful experience teaching Evidence. I would like to also thank my father, U.S. 6th Circuit Court of Appeals Judges James L. Ryan, for his inspiration and insight regarding the Federal Rules of Evidence.

This text is unique in that it provides "ready to use" materials for an entire fifteen-week law school Evidence or Advanced Evidence course and is designed for use by members of the judiciary and practitioners to assist them as a guide in finding answers to evidentiary issues that arise during trial; for law school professors to assist them in the preparation of their lectures and course materials; and for law students as a summary of Federal Rules of Evidence and in preparation for the bar examination as a review of the essential elements of the Federal Rules of Evidence.

This text is being also published for independent study credit supervised by Prof. James Richardson and in partial fulfillment of Doctor of Philosophy degree in Judicial Studies from the University of Nevada, Reno. I would like to dedicate this text to my wife, Mary Catherine, and our seven children.

LECTURE I

▼

EVIDENTIARY FRAMEWORK

1) **Introduction:**

   a) Eleven Hour Clock

   b) Four Questions:

      i) Do the rules apply?

        (1) Rules apply in all court proceedings (FRE 101) except as provided by statute, FRE 104, or in grand jury, extradition, sentencing, probation, warrant and bail proceedings as set forth in FRE 1101. Privileges apply in all proceedings.

      ii) Is the evidence relevant? (FRE 401, FRE 402)

      iii) Although relevant, should the evidence be excluded for some other reason?

      iv) Is the evidence credible or reliable?

2) **Topic One: An Evidence Framework**

   a) Definition of Evidence

   b) Three Substantive Qualities of Evidence

3) **Topic Two: Trial Management Tools**

    a) FRE 611(a): Control manner, method, and means of questioning as well as presentation of witnesses and evidence.

    b) FRE 102: Purpose and Construction: Rules interpreted to achieve fairness, avoid expense or delay.

    c) FRE 104(a): Preliminary Questions of Fact: Preliminary questions of admissibility are determined by the judge and the judge is not bound by the rules of evidence except as it relates to privilege.

    d) FRE 104(b): Conditional Relevancy

    e) FRE 103: Characterizing Evidence

        i) General rule: A timely and specific objection or motion to strike is required to preserve error. Offer of proof needed to preserve error if evidence excluded. Harmless Error and Plain Error

        ii) Recent amendment to FRE 103

    f) FRE 201: Judicial Notice: A judge may take judicial notice of an indisputable fact generally known in the jurisdiction or if it is established from an accurate and reputable source whether a party requests it or not. A judge must take judicial notice if requested by a party and provided with necessary information. The party opposing judicial notice must have an opportunity to be heard. In a criminal case, judicial notice is permissive while in a civil case it is conclusive.

    g) FRE 105: Limited Admissibility: Upon request of counsel, a judge shall instruct jury on limited admissibility of evidence.

    h) FRE 106: Rule or "Doctrine of Completeness". When a writing or other part of a writing is offered, the balance of the writing may be admitted upon request at that time if justice and fairness requires.

    i)   Witness Procedure

        i)   FRE 603: Oath is required of all witnesses

        ii) FRE 615: Exclusion of Witnesses

    j)   FRE 614/FRE 706: Court Witnesses. Court may call witnesses and appoint experts.

    k)   FRE 705: Facts and Data Underlying Expert Opinions

4)   Topic Three: Effect of Rulings on Evidence

    a)   FRE 103: Substantial Right of a Party: Must impact upon a substantial right of the party or will be construed as harmless

        i)   Harmless Error: FRE 103(a)

        ii) Plain Error: FRE 103(d) can be raised at any time including on appeal even if objection not preserved at trial.

    b)   Objection to Admission of Evidence: Must be timely and specific

    c)   Objection to Exclusion of Evidence: Offer of proof

FEDERAL RULES OF EVIDENCE
11 HOUR CLOCK

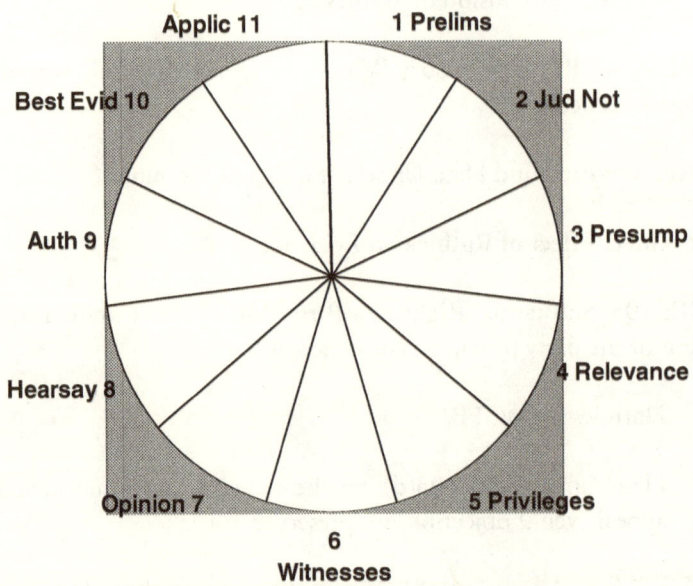

Four Questions:
1. Do the rules apply?
2. Is the evidence relevant?
3. Although relevant, should the evidence be excluded for some other reason?
4. Is the evidence credible or reliable?

LECTURE 2

▼

PRELIMINARY QUESTIONS OF FACT AND CONDITIONAL RELEVANCY

1) Introduction

   a) Rules of exclusion

   b) Examples

2) Foundational Facts Conditioning the Application of Technical Exclusionary Rules

   a) FRE 104: Judge determines preliminary questions of admissibility and is not bound by the rules of evidence except rules of privilege.

   b) General Rule

   c) Three examples: hearsay, competency of a witness, privilege

   d) Standard: Proponent must establish existence of the facts by a preponderance of the evidence. *Bourjaily v. United States, 483 U.S. 171 (1987)*

   e) Six Goals of FRE 104(a)

3) Foundational Facts Conditioning the Logical Relevance of the Evidence

   a) FRE 104(b)

b) General rule

c) Standard: Court simply examines the evidence in the case and decides whether the proponent has brought forth sufficient evidence from which a jury could reasonably find the existence of the conditional fact by a preponderance of the evidence. *Huddleston v. United States*, 485 U.S. 681 (1988).

d) Three problematic areas

    i) Constitutional privilege: Confessions

    ii) FRE 804(b)(2): dying declarations

    iii) Preliminary fact questions that go to the ultimate issue

4) Preliminary Factual Questions that go to the "Ultimate Issue"

5) Conclusion

LECTURE 3

▼

LOGICAL AND LEGAL RELEVANCY; UNFAIR PREJUDICE

I. **Topic One: Logical and Legal Relevancy; Unfair Prejudice**

A. Relevant Evidence

B. Definition: FRE 401. Evidence is admissible if it tends to make a consequential fact more or less probable. FRE 402 provides that relevant evidence is admissible unless excluded by other rule, statute, of the Constitution. Irrelevant evidence is inadmissible.

C. Logical Relevance

1. Must have a tendency

2. Must relate to a consequential or material fact:

a) "Materiality"

b) Does evidence make something in case more or less probable?

c) Must have some "probative value"

D. Legal Relevance

1. **FRE 404/FRE 405: Character.** Is generally not admissible to prove conformity therewith except that the defendant can place own character in issue, character of the victim, or character of a witness for truthfulness or untruthfulness. Other act evidence may not be introduced to show conformity but may be permissible for some other purpose such as motive, opportunity, intent, common scheme or plan, plan, etc.... Character may be proven by reputation or opinion. Specific instances of conduct are only admissible on cross unless character is in issue or an essential element of a claim or defense.

2. **FRE 406: Habit or routine practice:** If meets criteria, admissible to show conformity.

3. **FRE 407: Subsequent remedial measures**

   a) **Definition.** Not admissible to prove negligence, culpable conduct or defective product, but may be admissible for purposes to show feasibility, ownership, or to impeach.

   b) Rationale in negligence cases

   c) Rationale in strict liability cases

4. **FRE 408: Compromise and Offers**

   a) **Definition.** If a genuinely disputed claim, generally not admissible on validity of the tort claim but may be admissible for another purpose such as to show witness bias.

   b) Rationale

5. **FRE 409: Payment of medical and similar expenses.**

   a) **Definition.** Not admissible to prove liability

   b) Rationale

6. FRE 410: Pleas, discussions, statements

    a) Definition: Not admissible. Differs from FRE 408.

    b) Rationale

7. FRE 411: Liability insurance

    a) Definition: Generally not admissible to show fault but may be admissible to ownership or witness bias

    b) Rationale

8. FRE 412: Sex offense cases; relevance of victim's past behavior

    a) The rule: Generally not admissible with three exceptions: consent, source of semen or injury, or confrontation clause

    b) Rationale

II. Nature of relevant evidence

A. Direct Evidence

B. Circumstantial Evidence

III. Materiality

IV. Relevancy Analysis

V. Admissibility Analysis

VI. General Rule: FRE 402: Relevant Evidence is Generally Admissible and Irrelevant Evidence Inadmissible. Relevant evidence is admissible unless excluded by other rule, statute or constitution.

VII. Excluding Relevant Evidence

A. Various bases for exclusion (other than FRE 403)

B. The standard: FRE 403. Relevant evidence may be excluded if its probative value is substantially outweighed by danger of prejudice, confusion of the issues, misleading the jury or cumulative. Three administrative reasons and three policy reasons.

C. Checklist for excluding relevant evidence

    1. Unfair prejudice

    2. Confusion of the issues

    3. Misleading the jury

    4. Undue delay

    5. Waste of time

    6. Needless presentation of cumulative evidence

D. Balancing analysis

E. Limiting instruction?

    1. Application of the standard

F. Test for balancing probative value against harm under FRE 403: must "substantially outweigh"

G. Other tests which utilize FRE 403 for balancing probative value against harm: FRE 404(b), FRE 412, FRE 609 and FRE 703.

VIII. **Logical relevancy versus speculative or remote evidence**

A. Speculative evidence

B. Remote evidence

IX. Relevancy Distinguished from Sufficiency

1. The relevancy analysis under "law and economics analysis," the "likelihood ratio," and other "relevancy" standards

X. New Legal Relevancy Rules under the Federal Rules of Evidence

A. FRE 413: Defendant's prior act of sexual assault may be shown in prosecution for sexual assault

B. FRE 414: Defendant's prior act of child molestation may be shown in prosecution for child molestation

C. FRE 415: Prior acts admissible in **civil** matters involving allegations of sexual assault **or** child molestation

LECTURE 4

▼

CHARACTER AND HABIT

1) Character: In General. Inadmissible to show propensity except if the defendant puts own character in issue or attacks character of the victim, FRE 404(a)(1); or character of the victim in certain circumstances, FRE 404(a)(2); or character of a witness for truthfulness or untruthfulness, FRE 404(a)(3), FRE 607, FRE 608, FRE 609.

   a) For what purpose is the evidence of character being offered?

   b) What is the type of evidence offered to establish an individual's character? Pursuant to FRE 405 (a) character may be proven by reputation or opinion. Character may also proven by specific acts on cross-examination or when character is in issue. FRE 405(b)

2) Character in Issue: Specific instances of conduct are admissible when character is an essential element or is in issue. FRE 405 (b)

3) Character as Circumstantial Evidence: General Rules of Exclusion

4) Exceptions to the Rule of Exclusion

   a) Character for Care in Civil Cases

   b) Bad Character as Evidence of Criminal Conduct: Common Law and FRE 404(b): Other Acts or Crimes

    i) Doctrine of Completeness

    ii) Existence of a Larger Plan, Common Plan, Scheme or Conspiracy

    iii) Distinctive Device or signature crime

    iv) Absence of Mistake or Accident

    v) Motive

    vi) Opportunity

    vii) Malice, deliberation or requisite specific intent

    viii) Identity

    ix) Propensity for unusual or abnormal sexual relations: FRE 404(b); FRE 413; FRE 414; and FRE 415. May be demonstrated under traditional FRE 404(b) analysis or, under new rules, defendant's prior commission of sexual assault or child molestation may be shown in criminal (FRE 413; FRE 414) or by plaintiff in a civil case (FRE 415)

5) Impeachment of a witness by prior conviction: FRE 609

  a) The standard of proof

  b) The nexus between evidence and permissible purpose

    i) must be clear and must relate to a genuinely disputed

    ii) issue

  c) FRE 403 balancing test

6) Good Character as Evidence of Lawful Conduct: Proof by the Accused and rebuttal by the Government

7) Character in Civil Cases Where Crime is in Issue

8) Character of Victim in Cases of Assault, Murder and Rape

   a) Character of Victim: General Rule

   b) Character of Victim: FRE 412 and Sexual Assault Cases. Generally not admissible except three exceptions: consent, source of semen or injury, or confrontation.

9) Evidence of Character to Impeach a Witness: FRE 607, 608, 609

10) Habit and Custom as Evidence of Conduct on a Particular Occasion: FRE 406

11) FRE Amendment to FRE 404(a) effective 12-1-00: "Fair Play" Amendment

Ryan's Roadmap to Character Evidence

FRE 404: Character Evidence Not Admissible to Prove Conduct; Exceptions; Other Crimes

(a) Character Evidence Generally

(1) Character of the accused → 413
$\qquad\qquad\qquad\qquad\qquad$ 414
$\qquad\qquad\qquad\qquad\qquad$ 415

(2) Character of the Victim → 412

(3) Character of the Witness → 607
$\qquad\qquad\qquad\qquad\qquad$ 608
$\qquad\qquad\qquad\qquad\qquad$ 609

(b) Other crimes, wrongs or acts

LECTURE 5

▼

HABIT, CUSTOM AND SIMILAR HAPPENINGS

1) Introduction

   a) Legal relevancy

   b) General discussion of legal relevancy as it relates to habit evidence

2) FRE 406. Habit; Routine Practice. Evidence of a habit of a person or of the routine practice of an organization, whether corroborated or not and regardless of the presence of eyewitnesses, is relevant to prove that the conduct of the person or organization on a particular occasion was in conformity with the habit or routine practice.

3) Distinguishing character from habit

   a) Definition of Character

   b) Definition of Habit

   c) Definition of Custom

4) Two Questions:

a) Even if the conduct is shown to have occurred with frequency and regularity, is it the type of conduct that could constitute a habit? (Nature of the Act)

b) Even if it is the type of conduct that could constitute a habit, has sufficient evidence been produced to establish that the particular person or organization possessed the habit? (Sufficiency)

c) Cases:

i) *United States v. Mascio*, 774 F.2d 219 (7th Cir. 1985)

ii) *Lapierre v. Sawyer* 557 A.2d 640 (N.H. 1989)

iii) *DeLeon v. Kmart Corp.* 1998 W.L. 878078 (Ala. Civ. App. 1998)

iv) *Simplex v. Diversified Energy Systems*, 847 F.2d 1290 (7th Cir. 1988)

v) *Weil v. Seltzer*, 873 F.2d 1453 (D.C. Cir. 1989)

vi) *United States v. Holman*, 680 F.2d 1340 (11th Cir. 1982)

vii) *Meyer v. United States*, 638 F.2d 155 (10th Circ. 1980)

5) **Examples Distinguishing Character from Habit**

a) Two factors:

i) Specificity of conduct

ii) Frequency of the act

b) Examples

c) Cases:

i) *United States v. Troutman*, 814 F.2d 1428 (10th Cir. 1987)

        ii)   *United States v. Rangel-Arreola*, 991 F.2d 1519 (10th Cir. 1993)

        iii) *Howard v. Capitol Transit*, 97 F. Supp. 578 (D. D.C. 1951)

        iv) *Loughan v. Firestone Tire & Rubber*, 749 F.2d 1519 (11th Cir. 1985)

        v)   *Perrin v. Anderson*, 784 F.2d 1040 (10th Cir. 1986)

   d) Two factors to determine sufficiency

        i)   Frequency of the given behavior

        ii) Regularity of the behavior

        iii) Cases:

           (1) *United States v. Luttrell*, 612 F.2d 396 (8th Cir. 1980)

           (2) *Jones v. Southern Pacific R.R.*, 962 F.2d 447 (5th Cir. 1992)

6) **Policy considerations supporting the admissibility of habit and custom evidence**

   a) Greater probative value

   b) Potential for prejudice substantially less

   c) Unlikely to provoke sympathy or antipathy

7) **Discussion of the habit, custom, similar happenings of business organizations**

   a) General rules

   b) Cases

        i)   *Untied States v. Sheffield*, 992 F.2d 1164 (11th Cir. 1993)

        ii) *Rosenberg v. Linc.Am. Life Ins. Co.* 883 F.2d 1328 (7th Cir. 1989)

iii) *Wilson v. Volkswagen*, 561 F.2d 494 (4th Cir. 1977)

iv) *Anderson v. Malloy*, 700 F.2d 1208 (8th Cir. 1983)

v) *Griggs v. Firestone Tire & Rubber*, 513 F.2d 851 (8th Cir. 1975)

vi) *Muncie Aviation Corp. v. Party Doll Fleet*, 519 F.2d 1178 (5th Cir. 1975)

8) Foundational requirements

a) Foundational requirements

   i) Need to establish existence of habit or business custom but do not need corroboration or eyewitness

   ii) Conduct must be sufficiently particularized, frequent and regular to constitute a habit

   iii) The circumstances under which the habit or custom is followed must be present

b) FRE 403 limitations: *Perrin*, supra.

9) Methods to prove habit

a) Opinion: *Maynard v. Sayles*, 817 F.2d 50 (8th Cir. 1987)

b) Specific acts of conduct: *Weil*, supra.

10) Similar Acts

LECTURE 6

▼

RELEVANCY RULES IN SEX OFFENSE CASES

I. **Introduction**

II. **Legal and Logical Relevancy**

    A. Logical Relevancy

    B. Legal Relevancy

III. **Brief Review of General Rules Regarding Exclusion of Character Evidence**

    A. Character of victim (FRE 404 (a)(2) and FRE 412)

    B. Character of accused (FRE 404 (a)(1) and FRE 413, FRE 414, FRE 415)

IV. **Relationship between FRE 404 and FRE 412**

    A. FRE 404(a)

    B. FRE 412: Scope and purpose

    C. FRE 412: Relationship to character—criminal cases. Character of victim of a sexual assault not admissible to show conformity with three exceptions:

1. *United States v Messersmith*, 692 F. 2d 1315 (11th Cir. 1982)

C. Historical precedent for evidence of sex crimes prior to FRE 413, FRE 414 and FRE 415

    1. *State v Searle*, 239 P.2d 995 (Mont. 1952)

    2. *State v. Start*, 132 P.51 (Or. 1913)

    3. *State v. Williams*, 103 P.250 (Utah 1909)

    4. *State v. Jenson*, 455 P.2d 631 (Mont. 1969)

D. FRE 413

    1. The rule

    2. FRE 413: Scope. Defendant's prior act of sexual assault may be shown in prosecution for sexual assault

        a) *United States v. Guardia*, 135 F.3d 1326 (10th Cir. 1998)

    3. FRE 413: Burden of Proof

        a) *Huddleston v. United States*, 485 U.S. 681 (1988)

    4. FRE 413: Policy

    5. FRE 413: Procedural Requirements

E. FRE 414

    1. The rule: Defendant's prior act of child molestation may be shown in prosecution for child molestation.

    2. Comparison to FRE 413

    3. FRE 414: Policy

4. Prior history

   a) *United States v. Yellow*, 18 F.3d 1438 (8th Cir. 1994)

5. Procedural Requirements

   a) *United States v. LeCompte,* 131 F.3d 767 (8th Cir. 1997)

   b) *United States v. Larson,* 112 F.3d 600 (2nd Cir. 1997)

   c) *Huddleston, supra*

   d) *United States v. Meacham*, 115 F.3d 1488 (10th Cir. 1997)

   e) *United States v. McHorse*, 179 F.3d 889 (10th Cir. 1999)

F. FRE 415

1. FRE 415: The rule: Defendant's act of child molestation or sexual assault admissible in civil action alleging child molestation or sexual assault.

2. FRE 415: Scope

3. FRE 415: Procedural Requirements

VI. Conclusion

A. Constitutionality

1. *United States v. Enjady*, 134 F.3d 1427 (10th Cir. 1998)

B. Varying standard of proof among states

1. *Huddleston, supra*

2. *State v. Tharp*, 637 P.2d 961 (Wash. 1981)

3. *People v Albertson*, 145 P.2d 7 (Cal. 1944)

4.   *People v Golochowicz*, 319 N. W.2d 518 (Mich. 1982)

5.   *Commonwealth v. Donahue*, 549 A.2d 121 (Pa. 1988)

6.   *Tucker v. State* 412 P.2d 970 (Nev. 1966)

7.   *Cross v. State*, 386 A.2d 757 (Md. 1978)

C. Nexus and specificity

1.   *Golochowicz, supra*

2.   *United States v. Kendall*, 766 F.2d 1426 (10th Cir. 1985)

D. FRE 403 balancing

LECTURE 7

---▼---

PRIVILEGE, PRESUMPTIONS AND JUDICIAL NOTICE

1) **FRE: Privilege, Presumptions, and Judicial Notice**

   a) FRE 501: Privilege

   b) FRE 301 and FRE 302: Presumptions

   c) FRE 201: Judicial Notice

2) **Privilege**

   a) FRE 501: Privilege determined by common law except as provided by Constitution, statute or case law. If state law governs the case, state law governs privilege.

   b) Proposed Federal Rules but rejected prior to adoption:

      i) Required reports privileged by statute

      ii) Lawyer—client

      iii) Physician-patient

      iv) Psychotherapist-Patient

v) Spousal (adverse testimony/confidential communication)

vi) Communication to clergymen

vii) Political vote

viii) Trade secrets

ix) Secrets of state or other official information

x) Identity of informer

xi) Waiver of privilege by voluntary disclosure

xii) Privileged matter disclosed under compulsion or without opportunity to claim privilege

c) Federal created privilege: Accountant/Tax Preparer—Client. Tax Reform Act

d) Recent Supreme Court case: Vince Foster case. Attorney-client privilege survives death. *Swidler & Berlin v. United States*, 524 US 399 (1998)

e) Attorney-client privilege applies to corporate clients: *Upjohn v. United States*, 449 U.S. 383 (1981)

f) Privilege: Constitutional

i) Privilege against self-incrimination

ii) Confessions

iii) FRE 104(d) Testimony by accused: the accused does not by testifying at a preliminary matter become subject to x-examination as to other issues in the case.

iv) Privilege concerning improperly obtained evidence

v) Recent Supreme Court Privilege Cases: *Lilly v. Virginia, 527 U.S. 116 (1999)* (constitutional privilege/confrontation) and *Crawford v. Washington*, 2004 US Lexis 1838 (2004) (marital privilege/confrontation clause violation). Compare by analogy to *Bruton* and co-defendant statements.

3) Presumptions and Burdens of Proof

a) Concept partially codified in two Federal Rules of Evidence:

    i) FRE 301: Presumptions in General in Civil Actions and Proceedings. In civil cases involving federal law presumptions shift the burdens of going forward only and there is no shift in the burden of persuasion unless provided for by statute or court rule.

    ii) FRE 302: Applicability of State Law in Civil Actions and Proceedings. In cases governed by state law, presumptions involving the burden of going forward and the burden of persuasion are controlled by state law.

b) Burdens of Proof

    i) Burden of producing evidence: sufficiency regarding a particular fact in issue.

    ii) Burden of persuasion: persuading the trier of fact the fact is true

c) Allocating Burdens of Proof: No general rules but usually on the party who has pled a particular fact will have both the burden of production and persuasion. Several factors will determine including:

    i) The natural tendency to place the burdens on the party desiring change

    ii) Special policy considerations such as those disfavoring certain defenses

    iii) Convenience,

    iv) Fairness, and

    v) The judicial estimate of the probabilities.

d) Satisfying Burden of Producing Evidence

    i)   Needs to be more than a "scintilla"

    ii) The evidence must be such that a reasonable person could draw from it the inference of the existence of the particular fact to be proved.

    iii) "Evidence of such quality and weight that reasonable and fair minded men in the exercise of impartial judgment might reach different conclusions."

    iv) Issue: Should the burden of producing evidence vary depending on the required burden of persuasion. Some courts say no. Most courts say yes. Example: *Jackson v. Virginia*, 443 US 307(1979) ("whether a rational fact finder could have found the defendant guilty beyond a reasonable doubt.)

e) Satisfying Burden of Persuasion

    i)   Civil cases generally: "Proof that leads the jury to find that the existence of the contested fact is more probable than its nonexistence."

    ii) Clear or convincing evidence: An intermediate standard. Federal statute or the Constitution as interpreted by the US. Supreme Court has applied this standard to:

        (1) Cases involving commitment to a mental hospital,

        (2) Termination of parental rights,

        (3) Denaturalization and deportation.

        (4) Other cases in which intermediate standard has been applied:

            (a) Fraud and undue influence

            (b) Oral contracts to make a will and suits to establish terms of a lost will

            (c) Specific performance of an oral contract

(d) Proceedings to set aside, reform, modify written transactions, or official acts on grounds of fraud, mistake or incompleteness,

(e) Miscellaneous types of claims and defenses, varying from state to state, where there is thought to be special danger from deception or where the courts consider that the type of claim should be disfavored on policy grounds.

iii) Beyond a reasonable doubt: Criminal cases: Due process clause "protects the accused against conviction except upon proof beyond a reasonable doubt of every fact necessary to constitute the crime with which he is charges. *In re Winship*, 397 US 358,364 (1970).

(1) Applies to some "affirmative defenses":

(a) Self-defense

(b) Duress,

(c) Insanity

(d) Intoxication

(e) Claims that the accused is within an exception or proviso in the statute defining the crime.

(2) Sometimes the burden of producing is upon the defendant. Under certain circumstances, burden of persuasion may also shift to defendant relieving prosecution of proving the absence of the defense beyond a reasonable doubt. Creates both policy and constitutional problems.

4) **Presumptions:**

a) In general: FRE 301 indicates that in civil cases involving federal law presumptions shift the burdens of going forward only and there is no shift in the burden of persuasion unless provided for by statute or court rule. In cases governed by state law, presumptions involving the burden of going forward and the burden of persuasion are controlled by state law. A presumption is a standardized practice, under which certain facts are held to call for uniform treatment with respect to their effect as proof of other facts. Rules of law which are <u>not</u> presumptions: "conclusive presumptions", i.e. under 7 years old can't be convicted of felony, "presumption of innocence," and res ipsa loquitor

b) Reasons for creation and illustrative presumptions. Shifts burden of proof and may also assign burden of persuasion. There are 100's but most common examples:

   i)   Between connecting carriers, damage occurred on the line of the last carrier

   ii) Presumption of ownership from possession favoring the prior possessor lending stability to estates.

   iii) Presumptions dealing with survivorship of persons who died first without factual basis so that other rules of law may operate.

   iv) Actions of public officials including judicial proceeding are presumed to have been regularly and legally performed.

   v)   Letter properly addressed, stamped and mailed is presumed to have been duly delivered to the addressee

   vi) Negligent operation of vehicle: presumption driving within scope of agency.

   vii) Presumption that damage or loss of bailed goods was due to negligence or fault of bailee if bailor proves delivered in good condition and returned damaged or failure to return after demand.

   viii) Disappeared for 7 years with no contact with kin, presumption dead.

   ix) Presumption of identity of person from identity of name in tracing titles to land. When the same name in chain first as grantee/heir and then as grantor, it is presumed that it was same person.

x) Presumption of legitimacy of child born to married woman

xi) Presumption against suicide if violent death is shown but evidence is not controlling as to whether it was suicide or accident.

c) Constitutional Questions in civil cases

d) Presumptions in civil cases

e) Effect in civil cases

f) Constitutional questions in civil cases

g) Affirmative defenses and presumptions in criminal cases:

   i)   Terminology

   ii) Constitutionality

   iii) Special Problems

h) Choice of Law

i) Presumptions in *Civil* Cases

   i)   Thayer or Bursting Bubble theory: The only effect of a presumption is to shift the burden of producing evidence with regard to a presumed fact. If that evidence is produced by the adversary, the presumption is spent and disappears. Although a presumption is available to permit the party relying on it to survive a motion for directed verdict at the close of its case, it has no other value.

   ii) Thayer followed by majority of states, Wigmore, Model Code, and in part, FRE 301.

   iii) Deviations/Alternatives: Morgan Theory; Where the facts upon which the presumption is based have "probative value" the burden of persuasion is assigned to the adversary; where there is no such probative value, the presumption has only a "Thayerian" effect and dies when met by counterproof.

iv) FRE 301: In all civil actions and proceedings not otherwise provided for by Act of Congress or by these rules, a presumption imposes on the party against whom it is directed the burden of going forward with the evidence to rebut or meet the presumption, but does not shift to such party the burden of proof in the sense of the risk of non-persuasion, which remains upon the party on whom it was originally cast.

v) Burden of "persuasion" versus burden of "production"

vi) FRE 302. In civil actions and proceedings, the effect of a presumption respecting a fact which is an element of a claim or a defense as to which State law supplies the rule of decision is determined in accordance with State law. *Erie Railroad Co. v. Tompkins*, 304 U.S. 64 (1938)

j) Presumptions in *Criminal* Cases

i) Difference between affirmative defenses (insanity/self defense) and presumptions

ii) *County Court of Ulster v. Allen* 442 U.S. 140 (1979) (FF in vehicle, presumptive possession by all)

iii) Presumptions in criminal cases will be divided into mandatory and permissive presumptions. A permissive presumption is one that will permit the jury to find the presumed facts, but neither compels the acceptance of such facts nor allocates a burden of persuasion to the defendant with regard to those facts.

iv) Constitutionality of presumptions in criminal cases: Constitutionally acceptable if, considering all the evidence in the case, there is a "rational connection" between the basic facts proved by the prosecution and the ultimate fact presumed, and the latter is more likely than not to flow from the former.

5) **Judicial Notice: Adjudicative Facts.**

a) History: Bifurcation of roles. "To questions of fact judges do not answer: to questions of law the jury does not answer." Lord Coke.

b) FRE 201: Judicial Notice. In general, a judge may take judicial notice of an indisputable fact generally known in the jurisdiction or if it is established from an accurate and reputable source whether a party requests it or not. A judge must take judicial notice if requested by a party and provided with necessary information. The party opposing judicial notice must have an opportunity to be heard. In a criminal case, judicial notice is permissive while in a civil case it is conclusive

c) FRE 201 Scope: Limited to only adjudicative facts (States may differ and have broader application permitting judicial notice of law. Example: Michigan MRE 202)

d) Two (2) kinds of adjudicative facts:

   i) Generally known within the territorial jurisdiction of the trial court, or

      (1) ("Judicial notice may only be taken of those facts every damn fool knows." Dean McDermott)

      (2) Most common method,

   ii) Capable of accurate or ready determination by resort to sources whose accuracy is unquestionable.

      (1) Type 2 examples:

         (a) Judicial notice of scientific principles justifying evidentiary use of radar, blood tests for intoxication and non-paternity, handwriting and typewriter identification and ballistics. (Qualifications, reliability and weight still may be challenged.)

         (b) Historical facts

         (c) Geographical facts

         (d) State, local or national officials

      (2) Three (3) problems with type 2 judicial notice:

(a) Courts may fail to employ the doctrine of judicial notice in this field to the full measure of its usefulness

(b) Court may mistakenly accept or utilize as authoritative scientific theories that are outmoded or are not yet received by specialists as completely verified (Example, Roe v. Wade), or

(c) Courts in particular cases may misconceive the conclusions or applications that are supposed to flow from them.

e) Judicial Notice: Procedure

 i) When: If requested by a party and supplied with necessary information, it is mandatory. Otherwise, discretionary whether requested or not. May be taken at any time or stage of the proceeding.

 ii) Notice: Not generally required unless fact is less than obviously true.

 iii) Opportunity to be heard: Timely request on propriety or tenor of the matter. If no prior notification, may request after judicial notice taken.

 iv) Jury Impact:

  (1) Civil: Conclusive

  (2) Criminal: Jury may accept or reject

f) Judicial Notice: Legislative Facts

 i) Judicial notice of "legislative" facts: social and economic data used in judicial law making:

  (a) Examples: *Jay Burns Baking v. Bryan*, 264 US 504 (1924) (Nebraska legislature regulated weight and wrapping of bread to avoid misleading consumers regarding the size of bread. See Brandeis dissent.)

  (b) *Brown v. Board of Education*, 347 US 483 (1954) supplemented by 349 US 294.

ii) "Adjudicative" facts regulated by FRE 201, "legislative" facts not.

iii) Three problems with judicial notice of "legislative" facts in constitutional cases:

    (1) Historical and sociological data are so rehearsed that an opinion appears to be founded on purely pragmatic concerns rather than upon some constitutional norm.

    (2) Outpouring of learning disproportionate to the requirements of the problem at hand

    (3) Data may be an exercise in fustian excess, often in a losing cause.

g) Judicial Notice: Judicial Notice of Law Conference Commissioners on Uniform Law

    i) 1936: Uniform Judicial Notice of Foreign Law Act. Judicial notice of common law and statutes of every other state (principle of comity, adopted by half states)

    ii) 1962: Article IV of the Uniform Interstate and International Procedure Act addresses state but particularly foreign law and requires written notice (not widely adopted)

h) Law of Foreign Country: CL requires pleading and proof to jury. Jury decided what foreign law was like any other fact. 1936 Act requires pleading and proof of law of other nations to judge.

i) International and Maritime Law: Generally will take judicial notice unless maritime rules of foreign country which will be treated like foreign law requiring that they be proven unless published and accepted in this country as authentic foreign law.

j) Problems with requiring proof of foreign law:

    i) Proponent may not be able to prove foreign law leading to harsh and arbitrary results.

ii) Court may simply apply law of forum especially if parties have tried the case as if local law were applicable.

iii) May presume that the foreign law is the same as the forum particularly if the doctrine is one of common law unless the other nation is not a common law country. In that instance, court will decline to apply the presumption.

k) Judicial Notice of Law

i) Many states have adopted a Rule 202 to address problems governing judicial notice of law.

ii) Example: Michigan MRE 202: Judicial Notice of Law

(a) When Discretionary. A court may take judicial notice without request by a party of (1) the common law, constitutions, and public statutes in force in force in every state, territory, and jurisdiction of the United States; (2) private acts and resolutions of the Congress of the United States and of the Legislature of Michigan, and ordinances and regulations of governmental subdivisions or agencies of Michigan; and (3) the laws of foreign countries.

(b) When Conditionally Mandatory. A court shall take judicial notice of each matter specified in paragraph (a) of this rule if a party requests it and (1) furnishes the court sufficient information to enable it properly comply with the request and (2) has given each adverse party such notice as the court may require to enable the adverse party to prepare to meet the request.

(c) Rule based on 1953 version of Uniform Rules of Evidence by National Conference of Commissioners on Uniform State Laws.

LECTURE 8

▼

IMPEACHMENT AND REHABILITATION

1) **Introduction: Stages of impeachment/modes of attack**

   a) Six modes of attack upon credibility of a witness

   b) Two methods or stages of attack

   c) Cardinal rule

   d) Modern trend

2) **Prior inconsistent statement: Degree of inconsistency required**

   a) Warning unnecessary (FRE 613): Prior statements may be used without disclosing contents or source to witness but must show to attorney upon request.

   b) Opinion in form

   c) Extrinsic evidence permitted (FRE 613) if witness given an opportunity to explain or deny. Previous inconsistent statements as substantive evidence of the facts stated. FRE 801(d)(1)

   d) Requirement of preliminary questions on cross-examination as "foundation" for proof by extrinsic evidence. Extrinsic proof of prior inconsistent statement is inadmissible unless the witness is given an opportunity to explain. FRE 613

e) Rule against impeaching one's own witness (FRE 607): Anyone can impeach credibility of the witness even the party calling the witness. Surprise no longer required.

3) **Partiality/bias (FRE 401-3)** *U.S. v. Abel*, 469 U.S. 45 (1984)

4) **Character in general**

a) Misconduct, for which there has been no criminal conviction (FRE 608(b). The character for truthfulness or untruthfulness of a witness can be challenged on cross-examination as to specific acts. Character for truthfulness or untruthfulness can also be established through reputation of opinion witnesses. FRE 608(a)

b) Conviction of a crime (FRE 609). Evidence of prior conviction is admissible if a) it is a felony punishable by one year or more but subject to FRE 403 balancing, or b) if it involves dishonesty or false statement regardless of the penalty. False statement prong exempt from FRE 403 balancing. Subject to certain limitations such as time, i.e. ten years from date of conviction or release whichever is later, juvenile adjudication, appeal, etc.…

c) Impeachment by proof of opinion or bad reputation (FRE 608(a)). Character for truthfulness or untruthfulness can also be established through reputation of opinion

5) **Defects in capacity**

a) Presumption of competency (FRE 601). All persons presumed competent in federal court. In cases governed by state law, state law determines competency.

b) Lack of personal knowledge (FRE 602). Personal knowledge is required of all witnesses except experts.

c) Sensory deficiency: Inability to observe/remember/recount

d) Drug/alcohol use/mental disturbance

6) **Contradiction:** Not covered by any specific rules

   a) Devastating

   b) Often Noticed

   c) Limits

   d) Summary

   e) Waiver Issues

   f) Fairness Issues

   g) Constitutional Law (Criminal)

7) **Lack of religious belief (FRE 610):** Religious belief or lack of religious belief is inadmissible to impeach, to enhance, or to rehabilitate the credibility of a witness

8) **Rehabilitation/supporting witness**

   a) Can't bolster prior to attack (FRE 608)

   b) Can anticipate attacks

   c) Repair must meet or answer attack

   d) Good character: FRE 608(a) Opinion or Reputation

   e) Prior consistent statements (FRE 801(d)(1)(B))

      i)   Observation re: FRE 801 (d)(1)(B)

      ii) Pre-motive requirement: Interpreting *Tome v. U.S.*, 513 U.S. 150 (1995)

9) **Attacking the supporting character witness**

10) **Contradiction: collateral and non-collateral matters**

11) **Exclusion and sequestration of witnesses (FRE 615):** Court shall exclude witnesses upon request except a party or person whose presence is essential or authorized by statute.

12) **Pretrial Rulings and Preserving Error in Criminal Cases:** In criminal cases in which the Defendant may consider testifying, all claims of pretrial error may be waived if defendant chooses not to testify. *Luce v. United States*, 469 US 38 (1984) in which the Supreme Court ruled that failing to testify bars an appeal on the pretrial ruling that prior convictions may be used to impeach. States are split on the *Luce* doctrine. See also FRE 103 and its recent amendment.

▼

REAL AND DEMONSTRATIVE EVIDENCE: ADVANCED EVIDENTIARY ISSUES INVOLVING TRIAL TECHNOLOGY

Technology and Trial Practice

1) **Introduction**

   a) FRE 403

   b) Authentication

      i) FRE 901: Authentication. Evidence sufficient to demonstrate that document, object or thing is what the proponent claims it to be. FRE 901(b)(1) and FRE 901(b)(9) are of particular concern.

      ii) FRE 902: Self-Authenticating Documents. Do not need authenticating witness. Usually under seal such as government records, official publications, newspapers and periodicals, certified domestic and foreign business records, etc....

      iii) FRE 903: Subscribing witness not required under Federal Rules but may be required under state law

    c) Original Documents

        i)   Definition: FRE 1001

        ii) FRE 1002: Original required to prove its contents

        iii) FRE 1003: Duplicates permitted unless authenticity of original in dispute or it would be unfair.

        iv) FRE 1005: Contents of public record can be proven by certified copy. See FRE 902 for authentication.

        v)   FRE 1006: Summary of voluminous documents permitted. If requested original documents must be produced.

        vi) FRE 1007: Contents can be proven by testimony or affidavit

        vii) FRE 1008: Potential clash with FRE 104. FRE 1008 provides that the court decides preliminary facts (like FRE 104) but the jury decides whether original existed, and if two documents are produced which one is the original, and whether secondary evidence of the contents reflects the contents of the writing in dispute.

2)   The Use of Verdict/Trial Max or comparable litigation support

    a) Basic review of underlying technology and evidentiary foundational issues

    b) Documents

    c) Video depositions

3)   Real time court reporting

    a) Basic review of underlying technology and evidentiary foundational issues

    b) Traditional use (O.J. Simpson case)

    c) Case view (feed from court reporter to judge/attorneys/jurors)

4) **The effective use of PowerPoint or comparable presentation software during trial**

    a) Basic review of the underlying technology and evidentiary foundational issues

    b) Use during opening statement and closing arguments

    c) Demonstrative use with fact witnesses

    d) Scanning and importing sound, photographs, documents or diagrams

    e) Importing day in the life videos

    f) Use of Power Point or comparable technology by expert witnesses

        i) Scanning and importing photographs

        ii) Importing movies or videos

5) **The effective use of ELMO/Visualizer (or technological equivalent)**

    a) Basic review of underlying technology and evidentiary foundational issues

    b) Real tangible exhibits, i.e. gloves, knives, bullets, guns, currency, DNA sample

    c) Photographs (for traditional purposes and for impeachment purposes, i.e. eyewitness identification)

6) **Computer generated graphic video evidence**

    a) Basic review of underlying technology and evidentiary foundational issues

        i) Criminal

        ii) Civil

7) **Conclusion/Questions and Answers**

LECTURE 10

▼

HEARSAY

1) **Definition**: FRE 801. Hearsay is a statement, other than one made by the declarant (a person) while testifying at the trial or hearing, offered into evidence to prove the truth of the matter asserted.

   a) General definitions: OCSTMA

   b) "Out of court":

   c) "Truth of matter asserted"

      i)   Verbal or operative facts: Words of legal significance

      ii)   Verbal parts of acts, a.k.a. "res gestae": Conduct which accompanies words of legal significance

      iii) Statements manifesting awareness, i.e. prior knowledge

      iv)   States of mind: element or exception

      v)   Opinion surveys:

   d) "Statement." A statement includes an oral or written assertion or conduct intended as an assertion by the declarant. If not intended as an assertion, not hearsay.

i) Oral or written assertion: Hearsay

ii) Nonverbal or assertive conduct: Hearsay. Acts are statements if intended by the declarant to be an assertion.

iii) Silence in the face of accusation

iv) Non-assertive conduct

v) Assertions implied from other assertions

2) **The Rule**: FRE 802. Hearsay is inadmissible unless it meets some exclusion or exception set forth by rule or statute.

3) **Statements that are definitionally not hearsay: Prior statement by a witness**: FRE 801(d)(1). The declarant must 1) testify at trial, 2) be subject to cross-examination, and 3) the statement must be either:

a) Prior Inconsistent Statement. Made under oath at a prior proceeding may be admissible for impeachment purposes as well as for the truth of the prior matter. Compare to FRE 613 that is limited to impeachment only.

b) Consistent: if offered to rebut a charge of recent fabrication, improper influence or motive. Prior consistent statement must be made prior to motivation to fabricate exists. *Tome v. United States*, 115 S. Ct. 696 (1995).

c) Statement of prior identification

4) **Statements that are definitionally not hearsay: Admissions by party opponent**: FRE 801(d)(2). Party admissions are not hearsay if they are offered against a party and the statement is either:

a) Party's own statement

b) Adopted statement

c) Authorized statement (Requires additional corroboration)

d) Agent's statement (Requires additional corroboration), or

e) Co-conspirator's statement (Requires additional corroboration): *Bourjaily v. United States*, 483 U.S. 171 (1987)

f) The common law as to adopted, authorized and co-conspirator statements. The reliability rationale and the responsibility rationale.

g) Other admissions by a party opponent's which are not specifically covered by the Federal Rules

    i) Admissions by privities in estate, joint tenants, principals against surety, joint obligors, and predecessors in interest.

    ii) Admissions in pleadings

    iii) Admissions by conduct: flight and similar acts, failure to call witnesses or produce evidence, refusal to submit to medical examination, misconduct constituting obstruction of justice, offers to compromise (FRE 408) and plea bargain negations (FRE 410), safety measures after accident (FRE 407), offers to pay medical expenses (FRE 409)

5) **Exceptions: Availability of Declarant Immaterial FRE 803**. FRE 803 Policy Road Map

a) FRE 803(1) Present Sense Impression

    i) The rule: A present sense impression describing event made while observing the event or immediately thereafter is admissible. It need not be exciting but must be made while perceiving or immediately thereafter. If the declarant has the opportunity to reflect prior to making the statement, underlying policy consideration for the exception is undermined.

    ii) The foundational requirements

    iii) Examples

b) FRE 803(2): Excited Utterance:

i) The rule: An excited utterance relating to the startling event made while under the stress of the event is admissible. Need not be made immediately thereafter as long still under stress of the event and the statement is related to the starting event, i.e. coma, etc....

ii) The foundational requirements

iii) Examples

c) FRE 803(3): Then existing mental, emotional or physical condition:

   i) The rule: Statements regarding present mental, emotional, or physical condition are admissible including statements of intent or plan, but not statements of memory or belief except in probate or will and testament cases.

   ii) The foundational requirements

   iii) Examples

d) FRE 803(4) Statements made for purposes of medical diagnosis and treatments.

   i) The rule: Statements made for medical diagnosis or treatment that include history, and cause of condition, if medically necessary are admissible. Must be for medical diagnosis or treatment and extraneous statements not related to medical diagnosis or treatment are to be stricken unless they meet some other exclusion or exception. See FRE 805. Statements of identification are an issue as to whether they qualify as being pertinent to medical diagnosis or treatment.

   ii) The foundational requirements

   iii) Examples

e) FRE 803(5) Recorded recollection:

   i) The rule: A document made while the matter was fresh in the memory of the witness who now cannot completely remember may be admitted as the recorded recollection of the witness. If the document is admitted, it is read to the jury in lieu of testimony but is not received as an exhibit unless requested by the adverse party.

ii) The foundational requirements

iii) Examples: FRE 803(5)

iv) Refreshing recollection: FRE 612

    (1) The rule: Under FRE 612 anything including a writing, document or object, can be used to refresh recollection. A writing used to refresh recollection must be produced and the adverse party may introduce relevant parts into evidence.

    (2) Foundational requirements: FRE 612

    (3) Examples: FRE 612

f) FRE 803(6) Business Records

i) General Rule: Business records made and kept in the regular course of business are admissible. Custodian of the records or other qualified witness required to provide foundation which can now be done by affidavit under the FRE. Records prepared in anticipation of litigation are not business records.

ii) Foundational requirements

iii) 2000 Amendment provides for affidavit in lieu of live testimony. See FRE 902(11) and FRE 902(12). Authentication still required despite amendment.

iv) FRE 803(7) permits the absence of entries in a business record to show the non-occurrence or non-existence of a matter.

g) FRE 803(8) FRE 803(9), FRE 803(10), official records.

i) Underlying policy: inherent reliability

ii) FRE 803(8): Public Records and Reports which show the activities of the agency, or matters observed pursuant to duty, with exception of police officers or other law enforcement personnel in a criminal case, or findings of fact resulting from an investigation pursuant to legal authority or duty, except against a defendant in a criminal case, are admissible.

    (a) FRE 803(8): Foundational requirements

    (b) Differentiation from FRE 803(6): Usually self-authenticating.

    (c) Administrative investigative reports

    (d) Criminal case exclusion

iii) FRE 803(9): Records of Vital Statistics such as births, marriages or deaths are admissible as a hearsay exception.

iv) FRE 803(10) Absence of public record or entry are admissible to show non-occurrence or non-existence of a matter.

h) Miscellaneous Exceptions

  i) Learned Treatise: FRE 803(18)

    (1) The rule: A learned treatise is admissible if relied on during the direct or if utilized on cross-examination, or if it shown by testimony or judicial notice to be a reliable authority in the field. The treatise may be read into evidence but is not received as an exhibit.

    (2) Foundational requirements

    (3) Examples

  ii) Ancient documents: FRE 803(16). Statements in "ancient" documents are admissible if the document is 20 years or older and has been properly authenticated.

iii) Market reports, commercial publications: FRE 803(17) market reports and commercial publications of types relied upon by professionals or the public may be admissible.

iv) Family Records: FRE 803(13) such as Bibles, genealogies, or tombstones are also admissible. See also 803(12) which permits marriage and baptismal certificates and FRE 803 (19) which permits reputation testimony concerning personal or family history to show birth, marriage, death, relationship or similar matters. In addition to family records, records of religious organizations to show births, deaths, marriage and similar matters are also permitted under FRE 803(11).

v) Reputation concerning boundaries or general history: FRE 803(20) permits reputation testimony as to boundaries or historical matters if the reputation was established before the dispute arose. In addition to reputation evidence see also FRE 803(15) which permits statements affecting property interests in recorded documents if those statements are relevant and germane. FRE 803(14) also permits the admissibility of recorded documents affecting property interests as proof of content, execution, and delivery of the original.

vi) FRE 803(21) permits reputation as to character. Cross reference to FRE 405(a) and FRE 608(a).

vii) FRE 803(22) permits judgments of conviction of a felony to prove a fact essential to the judgment and judgments as to personal, family, general history or boundaries are permitted by FRE 803(23).

6) **Shift of FRE 803(24) to FRE 807 effective 12-1-97.** Compare to state codes.

7) **Exceptions. Declarant unavailable: FRE 804**

a) FRE 804(a): Definition of unavailability. A declarant is unavailable if they are dead, too ill, beyond ordinary process, disregards subpoena, lacks recollection, refuses to testify, or is exempt due to common law, statutory or constitutional privilege. Note of caution: a witness may be available if deposition can be taken.

b) FRE 804(b)(1) Former Testimony: Former testimony of a witness is admissible if the party against whom it is offered or a predecessor in interest in a civil case had an opportunity and similar motive to develop the testimony.

    i)   Policy: inherent reliability

    ii)   Foundational requirements

c)   FRE 804(b) (2) Statement of Impending Death or "Dying Declaration:" A statement of impending death is admissible if the declarant believed that death was imminent and the statement concerns the cause of death. Admissible in homicide and civil cases only.

d)   FRE 804(b)(3) Statement against pecuniary, proprietary, or penal interest may be admissible if at the time of making it was so far contrary to the declarant's interests that a reasonable person in the declarant's position would not have made such a statement unless they believed it to be true. Criminal case exception requires that statements exposing declarant to criminal liability and offered to exculpate the accused are not admissible unless corroborating circumstances clearly indicate trustworthiness of the statement.

    i)   General Rule

        (1) Against pecuniary interest

        (2) Against proprietary interest

        (3) Against penal interest

    ii)   Proposed but rejected 2002 amendment but see, *Lilly v. Virginia*, 527 U.S. 116 (1999); *Crawford v. Washington* (2004)

e)   Statement of personal or family history: FRE 804(b)(4). A statement concerning the declarant's birth, adoption, marriage, divorce, legitimacy, relationship by blood, adoption, or marriage, ancestry or similar fact of personal or family history is admissible if declarant is unavailable. Likewise, declarant's statements regarding a relative regarding those matters is also admissible if appears to be reliable and accurate.

f) Shift of FRE 804(b)(5) to FRE 807 and addition of new exception FRE 804(b)(6) Forfeiture by Wrongdoing on 12/1/97. The Forfeiture by Wrongdoing exception provides that a statement is admissible against the party who has wrongfully caused the declarant's unavailability. Compare to state codes.

8) **Hearsay within Hearsay**: FRE 805 Hearsay within hearsay may only be admitted if each level is either an exclusion or an exception

9) **Attacking and Supporting Credibility of Declarant**: FRE 806. If hearsay is admitted, the credibility of the declarant may be attacked and then supported or rehabilitated.

10) **The Residual Exception**: FRE 807

a) History and origin of rule and its amendment: FRE 803(24) and FRE 804(b)(5)

b) The current rule: A statement *not specifically covered by FRE 803 or FRE 804*, may be admissible if it has circumstantial guarantees of trustworthiness and pretrial notice provided by the proponent.

c) Requirements

i) Indicia of reliability: Equivalent circumstantial guarantees of trustworthiness

(1) Factors to be utilized in assessing the *reliability* of proffered statements:

(a) Nature of the statement (sworn or unsworn)

(b) Relationship between the declarant and the witness

(c) Knowledge and qualifications of the declarant

(d) Probable motivation of the declarant in making the statement

(e) Type of case (civil v criminal, jury v non-jury)

(2) Factors to be considered to determine trustworthiness:

    (a) Availability of the trustworthy evidence not encumbered by hearsay

    (b) Conditional admittance based upon extra-judicial consideration such as declarant's willingness to testify

ii) Statement must be offered as evidence of a material fact

iii) Statement must be more probative on the point for which it is offered than any other evidence that can be procured through reasonable efforts.

iv) Admission of the statement must be in accord with the general purposes of the rules and serve the interests of justice

v) Notice

d) Practical effect of the 5 requirements indicates that this exception should rarely if ever be used particularly where the precise language of the rule requires that the statement be "unanticipated by the other exceptions"

e) Major problem: 6th Amendment. Confrontation Clause

f) The Great Debate: Has the Residual Exception swallowed the hearsay rule?

11) Hearsay and the Confrontation Clause

a) *Ohio v. Roberts*, 448 U.S. 56 (1980) (former testimony)

b) *United States v Inadi*, 457 U.S. 387 (1986) (co-conspirator statement)

c) *Idaho v. Wright*, 497 U.S. 805 (1990) (residual clause)

d) *Illinois v. White*, 502 U.S. 346 (1992) (excited utterance, statement made for purposes of medical diagnosis or treatment)

e) *United States v. Ismoila*, 100 F3rd 380 (5th Cir. 1996) cert. den. 5-27-97 (business records, residual exception)

f) *Lilly v. Virginia*, 527 U.S. 116 (1999) (constitutional privilege/statement against penal interest) and *Crawford v. Washington*, 2004 US Lexis 1838 (2004) (marital privilege/statement against interest)

▼

THE OPINION RULE, EXPERTS AND EMERGING AREAS OF TESTIMONIAL EXPERTISE

I. The Evolution of the Rule Against Lay Opinion Testimony

    A. The English Common Law and Its Evolution (or De-evolution) in England and the United States: 1300-1850

    B. Judicial Response to the Exclusion of Lay Opinion Evidence: Attempts

        1. To Distinguish "Fact" from "Opinion"

           a) *Beech Aircraft v. Rainey*, 488 U.S. 153 (1988)

    C. The Consequences of the Judicial Attempts to Distinguish Between "Fact" and "Opinion"

    D. Judicial Erosion of the Prohibition of Lay Opinion Testimony

        1. Strict Necessity

           a) *Baltimore & Ohio Railroad Co. v Schultz*, 1 N.E. 324 (Ohio 1885)

           b) *Whitney v. Central Paper Stock*, 446 SW 2d 415 (Mo. App.1969)

      c)   *Beuttenmuller v. Vess Bottling Co.*, 447 S.W. 2d 519 (Mo. 1969)

      d)   *People v Reed*, 164 N.E. 847 (Ill. 1928)

      e)   *United States v. Yazzie*, 976 F.2d 1252 (9th Cir. 1992)

      f)   *Dulaney v. Burns*, 119 So. 21 (Ala. 1928)

      g)   *Pollard v. Rogers*, 173 So. 881 (Ala. 1937)

      h)   *City of Beaumont v. Kane*, 33 S.W. 2d 234 (Tex. Civ. App. 1930)

      i)   *State v. Morrow*, 541 S.W. 2d 738 (Mo. App. 1976)

      j)   *United States v. Timton*, 964 F.2d 650 (7th Cir. 1992)

E. Contemporary Standard: The Evolution of FRE 701. Lay opinion admissible if based on personal knowledge (FRE 602) and assists or is helpful to the trier of fact (FRE 401, FRE 402)

    1. *Allen v. Matson Navigation Co.*, 255 F.2d 272 (9th Cir. 1958)

    2. *Baltimore & Ohio R.R.*, *supra*

    3. *Government of the Virgin Islands v. Knight*, 989 F.2d 619 (3rd Cir. 1993)

F. Current Status and Proposals for the Opinion Rule and the Foundational

    1. Requirements for FRE 701

    2. Remove Lay Opinion as a Matter Governed by the Rules

    3. FRE 701: Admissible if based on personal knowledge (FRE 602) and is helpful to the trier of fact. (FRE 401, FRE 402)

    4. FRE 403. Lay opinion may be excluded if misleads or confuses the jury. Although lay witness permitted to give an opinion on ultimate issue under FRE 704, FRE 403 may still provided a basis to exclude.

    5. Examples of Admissible Lay Opinion Testimony

II. Lay and Expert Opinions on an Ultimate Issue: FRE 704

A. **FRE 704(a)**: Opinion on the ultimate issue may be properly given by an expert or lay witness.

1. Background and the rule

   a) *Grismore v Consolidated Products*, 5 N.W. 2d 646 (Iowa 1942)

2. Rules which may be utilized to exclude ultimate opinion testimony

   a) *Mitroff v. Xomox*, 797 F.2d 217 (6th Cir. 1986)

   b) *Kostelecky v. NL Acme Tool/NL Industries, Inc.* 837 F.2d 828 (8th Cir. 1988)

3. Ultimate opinions on questions of law or mixed questions of law and facts

   a) *State v. Grimes*, 561 A.2d 647 (N.J. Super. 1989)

   b) *Andrews v. Metro North Commuter R. Co.* 882 F.2d 705 (2nd Cir. 1989)

   c) *Terrell v. Reinecker*, 482 N.W. 2d 428 (Iowa 1992)

   d) *Behlke v. Conwed Corp.* 474 N.W. 2d 351 (Minn. App. 1991)

   e) *Armstrong v. State* 826 P.2d 1106 (Wyo. 1992)

   f) *Hines v. Denver & Rio Grande Western R.*, 829 P.2d 419 (Colo. App. 1991)

   g) *Puente v. ASI Signs*, 821 S.W. 2d 400 (Tex. App. 1991)

   h) *Jones v. Garnes*, 395 S.E. 2d 548 (W.V. 1990)

   i) *State v. Larsen*, 828 P.2d 487 (Utah App. 1992)

   j) *Metot v. Danielson*, 780 SW 2d 283 (Tex. App. 1989)

B. **The Hinckley Exception:** FRE 704(b) An expert is precluded from testifying regarding the mental state or condition of a defendant in a criminal case and giving an opinion as to whether the defendant did or did not have the mental state or condition which constitutes an element of the crime charge or a defense to the crime charged. In this instance only, the ultimate issue of mental state or condition is left to the trier of fact alone.

1. *United States v. Brawner*, 471 F.2d 969 (DC Cir. 1972)

2. *United States v. Thigpen*, 4 F.3d 1573 (11th Cir. 1993)

3. *United States v. Frisbee*, 623 F. Supp. 1217 (N.D. Cal, 1985)

III. **FRE 702: Daubert and Beyond**

A. **Introduction:** Frye's general acceptance and other standards employed to evaluate the admissibility of expert opinion testimony has been replaced by Daubert's relevance and non-exclusive reliability standard. A qualified expert's opinion is admissible if reliable and helpful to the trier of fact. The new FRE 702 formula: **Qualifications + (relevance + reliability) = admissibility.**

1. *Coleman v. Parkline Corp.*, 844 F2d 863 (DC Cir. 1988)

B. **Proper subject for expert inference or opinion**

1. *United States v. Downing*, 753 F.2d 1224 (3rd Cir. 1985)

2. *State v Chapple*, 660 P.2d 1208 (Ariz. 1983)

3. *People v McDonald*, 690 P.2d 709 (Cal. 1984)

4. *Scott v. Sears, Roebuck*, 789 F.2d 1052 (4th Cir. 1986)

C. **The witness's qualifications as an expert**

1. *Caisson Corp. v. Ingersoll-Rand Co.*, 622 F.2d 672 (3rd Cir. 1980)

D. **The validity of the expert's underlying theory or technique: Daubert and its progeny**

1. *Frye v. United States*, 293 F. 10103 (D.C. Cir. 1923)

2. FRE 702 to *United States v. Downing, supra*

3. *Daubert v. Merrell Dow*, 113 S. Ct. 2786 (1993) and its progeny

4. **Ryan,** *Expert Opinion Testimony and Scientific Evidence: Does MCL 600.2955 "Assist" the Trial Judge in Michigan Tort Cases?* **75 Univ. of Det-Mercy L. Rev. 263 (1998)**

5. **Ryan,** *Michigan Rule of Evidence 702: Amend It or Leave It To Schanz?* **19. T.M.Cooley L. Rev. 1 (2002)**

6. *General Electric v. Joiner*, 118 S. Ct. 512 (1997)

7. *Kumho Tire v. Carmichael*, 119 S. Ct. 1167 (1999)

E. **Trustworthiness of the expert's minor premise**

F. **Cross-examination of experts**

1. The impact of FRE 705 on cross-examination. An expert may state an opinion without first providing the underlying facts unless the court requires otherwise. Underlying facts providing the basis of the expert's opinion may be explored on cross-examination.

2. The use of "learned treatises" FRE 803(18) and other published material. An expert may use a learned treatise on direct or utilized on cross-examination as long as it has been shown by testimony or judicial notice to be reliable. The learned treatise may be read into evidence but is not received as an exhibit and is not permitted into the jury room.

3. Establishing bias through financial interest

    a) *Sears v. Ritishauser*, 466 N.E. 2d 210 (Ill. 1984)

4. Scope and Judicial Discretion

IV. **The grounds for expert opinion**

    A. The hypothetical question

        1. The general rule: Permitted as long as it does not assume facts not in evidence

        2. Should the hypothetical question be retained in light of FRE 703 and FRE 705?

V. **The expert's opinion based on reports of others, inadmissible evidence, or data and facts which have not been admitted.**

    A. The general rule: An expert's opinion may be based on admissible or inadmissible evidence as long as these facts would be reasonably relied upon by experts in the field. If the evidence would be otherwise inadmissible, the proponent may not introduce the evidence unless the judge employs a FRE 403 balancing analysis.

    B. The substantive question under FRE 703

    C. The procedure for administering FRE 703

    D. Amendment of FRE 703 and FRE 403 balancing analysis.

VI. **Proposals for the improvement of the practice relating expert testimony and FRE 706:** Court may appoint expert witnesses and compensate them appropriately. It is important to follow the rule regarding appointment. The mutual selection of a court appointed expert can be utilized as an alternative dispute resolution method

LECTURE 12

▼

RECENT AND PROPOSED AMENDMENTS TO THE FEDERAL RULES OF EVIDENCE

I. **1997 Amendments**

   A. FRE 801(d)(2)(C)(D)(E): Corroborating Circumstances Requirement

   B. FRE 803(24): Transferred to FRE 807

   C. FRE 804(b)(5): Transferred to FRE 807

   D. FRE 804(b)(6): Forfeiture by wrongdoing

   E. FRE 807: Residual Exception

II. **2000 Amendments**

   A. FRE 103: Ruling on Evidence

   B. FRE 404: Fair Play Doctrine

   C. FRE 701: Opinion Testimony

   D. FRE 702: Testimony by Experts

E. FRE 703: Basis of Opinion Testimony by Experts

F. FRE 803(6): Business Records

G. FRE 902(11) and FRE 902(12): Self Authentication

III. Proposed Amendments: June 2002

A. FRE 608: Character and Conduct of Witness

B. FRE 804(b) (3): Statement against Interest (Not adopted)

978-0-595-36554-8
0-595-36554-X